~ FiRST GREEK MYTHS ~
JASON AND THE GOLDEN FLEECE

For Phil Fluke
S.P.

To all my boys
J.L.

ORCHARD BOOKS
338 Euston Road, London NW1 3BH
Orchard Books Australia
Level 17/207 Kent Street, Sydney NSW 2000
This text was first published in the form of a gift collection
called *First Greek Myths* by Orchard Books in 2003
This edition first published in hardback by Orchard Books in 2008
First paperback publication in 2009
Text © Saviour Pirotta 2008
Cover illustrations © Jan Lewis 2008
Inside illustrations © Jan Lewis 2008
The rights of Saviour Pirotta to be identified as the author and
of Jan Lewis to be identified as the illustrator of this work
have been asserted by them in accordance with the
Copyright, Designs and Patents Act, 1988.
A CIP catalogue record for this book is available from the British Library.
ISBN 978 1 84616 475 0 (hardback)
ISBN 978 1 84616 773 7 (paperback)
1 3 5 7 9 10 8 6 4 2 (hardback)
1 3 5 7 9 10 8 6 4 2 (paperback)
Orchard Books is a division of Hachette Children's Books,
an Hachette Livre UK company.
Printed in China

www.orchardbooks.co.uk

~ FIRST GREEK MYTHS ~
JASON AND THE GOLDEN FLEECE

BY SAVIOUR PIROTTA
ILLUSTRATED BY JAN LEWIS

ORCHARD BOOKS

~ CAST LIST ~

PRINCESS MEDEA
(Med-ey-ah)

PRINCE JASON
(Jay-sun)

In the faraway kingdom of Colchis lived a beautiful princess called Medea. She had magic powers.

Life was very dull on Colchis. Medea wished she lived somewhere more exciting.

One day Medea saw a ship, the *Argo*, sail into the harbour. The captain was Jason, Prince of Greece. Jason had led his brave sailors, the Argonauts, through many dangers.

"Greetings," Jason called. "We are here to find the treasure, the Golden Fleece, and carry it back to Greece. Then my wicked uncle will give back the throne to my father, who is the rightful king."

Princess Medea smiled. Here was her chance to leave Colchis. There was just one problem.

"My father, the king, will never let you take the Golden Fleece," she said. "He believes it brings us good luck. But I could help you."

Medea took Jason to see the king.
"Father," she said. "These men
have come in search of the
Golden Fleece."

10

"Very well," said the king. But
he wasn't worried. Many brave
men had tried to take the treasure.
All of them had died trying.

"You must sow these seeds in the field behind my palace," the king said. "Catch!" He threw Jason a leather bag.

"Be careful," Princess Medea warned. "Those seeds are dragons' teeth. If anything comes out of the ground, throw a rock at it."

Jason did as the king had asked
and scattered the dragons' teeth
around the field.

Suddenly, the ground started to shake. Skeleton hands reached out of the earth and Jason was surrounded by an army of evil-looking soldiers.

15

Jason fought well, but there
were too many skeletons. Then he
remembered Medea's warning. He
ducked between the soldiers' legs
and ran to the side of the field.

He picked up a boulder and threw it at the soldiers. The army scattered, and the bones fell to the ground.

The king frowned when he saw Jason back in the palace. Now he would have to let him try and get the Golden Fleece.

"There is worse to come, Jason,"
whispered Medea. "The Golden
Fleece is guarded by a serpent
that never sleeps."

"The serpent can only be tricked by magic," Medea went on. "But I will help you again if you promise to take me away with you to Greece."

"I'll do anything you ask," Jason promised.

"Then, when the serpent attacks, hold this magic flower under its nose," said Medea.

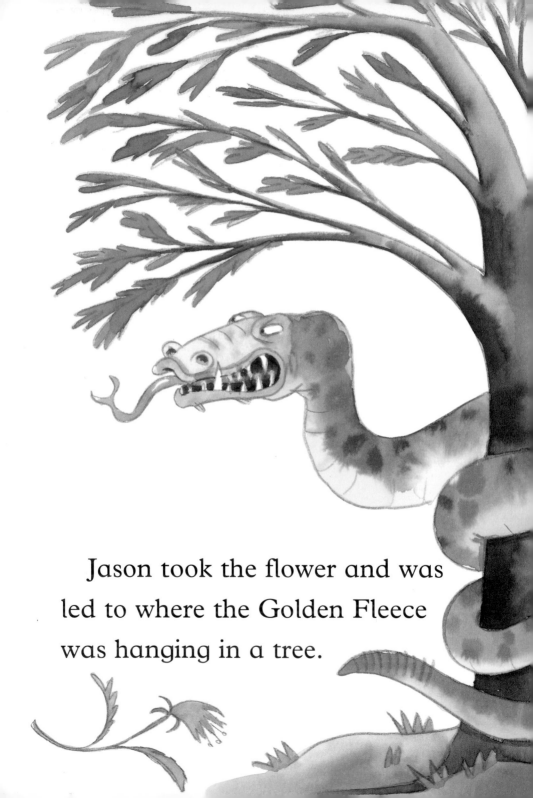

Jason took the flower and was led to where the Golden Fleece was hanging in a tree.

The giant serpent was wrapped
around its trunk.

Jason handed his sword to
Medea and walked forward.

The Argonauts shivered. Soon
Jason would be within the
serpent's deadly reach.

Calmly, he took Medea's flower and waved it under the serpent's nose. The monster breathed in the scent. Its head thudded to the ground and it began to snore.

Carefully, Jason stepped over
its scaly body and grabbed the
Golden Fleece.

The Argonauts cheered and
sped back to the harbour.

The *Argo* set sail for Greece
with a very happy Jason and an
even happier Princess Medea.

Princess Medea's father sent
his ships to recapture the Golden
Fleece but Medea whipped up
a fog and hid the *Argo*.

At last the powerful princess
was free.

~ FIRST GREEK MYTHS ~
JASON AND THE GOLDEN FLEECE
BY SAVIOUR PIROTTA ~ ILLUSTRATED BY JAN LEWIS

And enjoy a little magic with these First Fairy Tales:

First Greek Myths and First Fairy Tales are available from all
good bookshops,or can be ordered direct from the publisher:
Orchard Books, PO BOX 29, Douglas IM99 1BQ
Credit card orders please telephone 01624 836000
or fax 01624 837033
or e-mail: bookshop@enterprise.net for details.

To order please quote title, author and ISBN
and your full name and address.
Cheques and postal orders should be
made payable to 'Bookpost plc'.
Postage and packing is FREE within the UK
(overseas customers should add £1.00 per book).

Prices and availability are subject to change.